Step by Step

Wok

Step by Step

Wok

Susan Brazel

Bloomsbury Books
London

Page 2: Chicken and Mango Stir-Fry (p. 21) and mangetout (snow peas) make a delicious meal served with steamed rice and Chinese tea. The preparation is shown on the endpapers.

This edition published in 1994 by
Bloomsbury Books
an imprint of
The Godfrey Cave Group
42 Bloomsbury Street, London. WC1B 3QJ
under license from
Harlaxton Publishing Limited

Harlaxton Publishing Limited
2 Avenue Road, Grantham, Lincolnshire, NG31 6TA
United Kingdom
A Member of the Weldon International Group of Companies

First Published in 1994

Publisher: Robin Burgess
Project Coordinator: Barbara Beckett
Designer: Rachel Rush
Edited by: Alison Leach
Illustrator: Amanda McPaul
Jacket photographer: Rodney Weidland
Inside photography: Andrew Elton
Food styling assisted by John Fenton-Smith
Produced by Barbara Beckett Publishing
Colour Separation: G.A. Graphics, Stamford, UK
Printer: Imago, Singapore
Produced by Barbara Beckett Publishing

British Library Cataloguing-in-Publication data.
A catalogue record for this book is available from the British Library

Title: Step by Step, WOK
ISBN: 1 85471 392 2

Contents

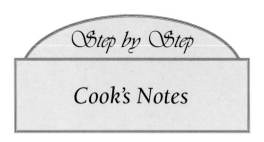

Cook's Notes

Measurements

All spoon and cup measurements are level. Standard spoon and cup measures are used in all the recipes. I recommend using a graduated nest of measuring cups: 1 cup, ½ cup, ⅓ cup and ¼ cup. The graduated nest of spoons comprises 1 tablespoon, 1 teaspoon, ½ teaspoon and ¼ teaspoon. For liquids, use a standard litre or imperial pint measuring jug, which also shows cup measurements. As the metric/imperial/US equivalents given are not exact, follow only one system of measurement within the recipe.

Ovens should be preheated to the specified temperature. When cooking on the hob (stoveplate), use medium heat where high, low or simmer are not specified.

Ingredients

Fresh **fruit** and **vegetables** should be used in the recipes unless otherwise stated. **Herb** quantities are for fresh herbs; if fresh are unavailable, use half the quantity of dried herbs. Use freshly ground black **pepper** whenever pepper is listed; use **salt** and pepper to individual taste. Use plain (all–purpose) **flour** unless otherwise stated. Fresh **ginger** should be used throughout, unless ground ginger is called for. Use fresh **chillies**; if substituting dried chillies, halve the quantity. If a recipe does not call for a specific type of oil, use a vegetable oil. Preferably use fermented wine vinegar; however cider vinegar and malt vinegar may be substituted if preferred. White granulated **sugar** is used unless otherwise stated.

This Stir-Fried Chicken Teriyaki (p. 22) is especially good because of the combination of vegetables. The mangetout (snow peas), bamboo shoots and spring onions (scallions) not only add colour, but a delicious crispness to the finished dish.

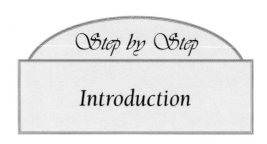

Introduction

The wok originated in China. It is now the main cooking utensil in a number of Asian countries as well as being used in many Western countries because of the unique way in which it cooks food. In Indonesia the wok is called a 'kuali' or 'wajan', the Malay version is also a 'kuali', and in Vietnam it is called a 'chao'. It is a cooking pan that is shaped like a large bowl with a rounded base. The base was rounded so that it fitted into the large open fires that were used for cooking. Today there are a variety of woks available. There are those with flat bases that are best suited to electric hotplates and electric woks with the element built into the base of the wok. The general shape is the same in all woks, the wide open area being perfect for quick, even cooking of food.

The wok is one of the most versatile pieces of cooking equipment available. It can be used for stir–frying, deep-frying, steaming, braising and boiling. For someone just beginning to set up a kitchen, it is a great investment. The best woks are often inexpensive, and the more a wok is used, the better it is to cook in.

Before using a new wok it is important to season it. First it should be well washed with hot water and detergent to remove any coating that the wok may have on it. If the coating is a lacquer type, fill the wok with cold water together with a couple of tablespoons of bicarbonate of soda (baking soda) and boil it for 15 minutes before removing the coating with a fine scourer. The wok is then ready to be seasoned. To do this, place your wok over the heat, pour in a couple of tablespoons of oil, add some chopped spring onions (scallions) and garlic cloves, then stir–fry these ingredients over moderate heat for 2–3 minutes, covering the whole wok surface. Throw out the mixture and wash the wok in warm water. Wipe the wok out with paper towels and rub a fine film of oil over the inside. After seasoning a wok, never use anything abrasive to clean it. After every use, fill the wok with water, then wash it in soapy water. Always dry the wok well and wipe it out with a little oil before storing.

Cooking in a wok is good for quick family meals. It is also great for entertaining, because with stir–frying most of the work is in the preparation and this can all be done in advance before the guests arrive.

This book will teach you the basic steps in preparing food that can be cooked in the wok. It will also help you with techniques you may not have tried before or are a little nervous about.

The instructions are clearly set out. There are step-by-step guides to different cooking methods such as stir–frying, deep-frying, steaming and braising. Many of the recipes are photographed in preparation stages to illustrate a special technique, to show you what the finished dish looks like and how to present it for the table. Detailed step-by-step drawings show you how to prepare vegetables for quick cooking, how to prepare crabs and how to make dim sim.

A glossary of cooking terms is on page 48 for you to look up any term that is unfamiliar. There

All the ingredients for Oriental French Bean Stir-Fry (p. 11)—crisp, young beans, sesame oil and soy sauce.

is a list of recipes on page 5 for your reference. Be sure to read the information on measurements and ingredients on page 6.

One of the most important things to do when trying a new recipe is to read the recipe very thoroughly before starting. Check that you have all the ingredients, and make an estimate of the amount of time needed. Have you time to braise the beef? Or would it be better to do a quick stir-fry?

The recipes are from a variety of Asian cuisines plus a selection of recipes that translate well to wok cooking.

Tenderizing Meat Chinese Style

The Chinese often use the following method to make the cheaper cuts of lean meat more tender. This meat can then be used for the quick cooking stir–fried dishes. Follow the directions in the recipe either to slice the meat or cut it into strips, then for every 450 g/1 lb of meat, dissolve 1/2 teaspoon of bicarbonate of soda (baking soda) in 3 tablespoons of hot water. Add to the meat and mix well until the meat has absorbed all the liquid. Cover and chill for at least 2 hours or even overnight. Proceed with the recipe as usual.

Step by Step

Stir-Frying

The rounded shape and the high, wide sides of the wok make it ideal for stir–frying. You can toss and stir–fry all the ingredients without having them jump out of the pan and all over the kitchen.

As the wok is made from thin iron, it heats up quickly and you get the fierce heat which is so necessary for this type of cooking, as it seals the food quickly and retains the juices. The Chinese introduced stir–frying as a means of conserving fuel: as the pieces of food are small, cooking time is usually only a few minutes.

Stir–frying uses very little oil or fat. It is the fierce heat and speed of cooking combined with properly cut ingredients which produce the wonderful crisp texture that is characteristic of stir–fried dishes. Stir–fried vegetables are especially nutritious because of the small amount of oil required and the quick cooking which ensures that most of the nutrients found in the vegetables are retained. It also does wonders for the colours, keeping them bright and clean.

With all stir–fried dishes it is the preparation that is important. Make sure that everything is ready before you start to heat the oil. Vegetables of all kinds should be cut to about the same size. Those that have a firmer texture, such as broccoli should be cooked first, and softer textures such as mushrooms should be added towards the end of the cooking.

Good-quality tender cuts of meat and poultry are best for stir–frying; the meat is quickly sealed and cooked to retain the maximum amount of moisture. The meat should be cut into evenly sized pieces. Meat cut across the grain will produce tender strips that will not toughen during the cooking. To cut meat or chicken into these strips for stir–frying, it is often a good idea to freeze the meat partially first, as it is much easier to hold and handle in this state.

Any type of edible oil can be used for stir–frying. Traditionally the Chinese used peanut oil, which can be heated to a high temperature without burning, often adding some sesame oil for flavour. If spices or flavourings such as garlic, ginger or chilli are used, these are often quickly stir–fried in the hot oil before the other ingredients are added.

Always heat the wok before adding the oil, then heat the oil before adding the food. This prevents the food from sticking.

Some of the stir–fry recipes may appear quite long, but do not let this deter you. Once the preparation is complete, the actual stir–frying of the ingredients is usually very quick.

Toasting Sesame Seeds or Nuts

Sesame seeds or nuts that are toasted before being used in a recipe have a nuttier, more flavoursome taste. The seeds or nuts can be placed on a baking sheet and toasted under a heated grill (broiler).

Toasted sesame seeds and flaked (slivered) almonds add the finishing touch to Oriental French Bean Stir-Fry.

Oriental French Bean Stir-fry

Use whole baby French (green) beans for this dish and serve it as an entrée or a vegetable accompaniment. A delicious variation is to use fresh young asparagus when it is in season instead of the beans.

1 tablespoon sesame oil
500 g/18 oz baby French (green) beans
2 teaspoons light soy sauce

2 teaspoons toasted sesame seeds
2 tablespoons toasted flaked (slivered) almonds
1 spring onion (scallion), thinly sliced

Heat the wok and pour in the oil. Add the beans and stir–fry for 1–2 minutes before adding the soy sauce, sesame seeds, almonds and spring onion. Continue to stir–fry a further minute. Serve immediately.
Serves 2–4

Stir-Frying

Heat the wok, then heat the oil and add the marinated meat pieces. Stir-fry until colour changes. Remove.	Add the cut vegetables and stir-fry for several minutes.	Return the meat to the wok and continue to stir-fry.	Add the sauce, stir until it has thickened and serve immediately.

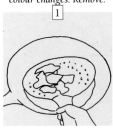 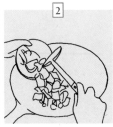  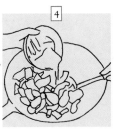

Stir-Fried Vegetable Medley

A bright, colourful combination of vegetables that are both crisp and nutritious. Vary the vegetables to include your favourites.

4 spring onions (scallions)
2 carrots
1 courgette (baby marrow, zucchini)
1 red pepper (capsicum, bell pepper)
1 green pepper
1 celery stick

125 g/4 oz French/1 cup sliced (green) beans
125 g/4 oz/2 cups sliced mushrooms
1–2 tablespoons oil
1 garlic clove, chopped
1 piece of fresh root ginger (2.5 cm/1 inch), grated
1 chilli, chopped

Prepare the vegetables by cutting the spring onions, carrots, courgette and peppers into julienne strips (p. 13) and the celery into diagonal slices.

Heat the wok and pour in the oil. Add the garlic, ginger and chilli and stir–fry for 30 seconds before adding the vegetables. Continue to stir–fry, moving the vegetables all around the pan, for 3–4 minutes. Serve immediately.
Serves 4

Garlic Bok Choy

Bok choy is a Chinese leaf vegetable that has a delicate flavour and a rich green colour. It makes a great addition to stir-fried vegetable dishes and is good served on its own, as in this dish.

1 tablespoon peanut oil
1 teaspoon sesame oil
1 garlic clove, chopped

1 bunch bok choy, sliced
1–2 tablespoons teriyaki sauce

Heat the wok and add the peanut oil and sesame oil, stir in the garlic and bok choy. Stir–fry over a high heat for 2–3 minutes. Stir in the teriyaki sauce just before serving. Serve immediately.
Serves 4

Lettuce Rolls (Sarng Choy Bao)

A popular Chinese dish served in lettuce, rolled and eaten with the fingers. This makes a great starter, both for the meal and the conversation.

60 g/2 oz/½ cup dried mushrooms
1 tablespoon oil
225 g/8 oz/2 cups minced (ground) pork
6 water chestnuts, chopped
3 tablespoons chopped bamboo shoots
175 g/6 oz can crab meat

6 spring onions (scallions), chopped
2 teaspoons sesame oil
1 tablespoon soy sauce
2 teaspoons oyster sauce
2 tablespoons dry sherry
1 round leaf (lettuce)

Soak the mushrooms in cold water for 30 minutes or until soft. Drain them and chop them finely. Heat the wok and add the oil. Stir in the minced pork and cook over a high heat for 3–4 minutes or until the pork changes colour. Add the water chestnuts, bamboo shoots, crab meat, spring onions, sesame oil, soy sauce, oyster sauce and dry sherry. Stir–fry the mixture over a high heat until the ingredients are heated through and well mixed together.

To prepare the lettuce cups, separate lettuce leaves, trimming larger leaves into rounds. Place the leaves on an upturned Chinese serving bowl and place a second bowl on top of the lettuce. Now immerse the bowls in cold water to crisp the lettuce until ready to serve. Before serving, drain the lettuce cups and pat them dry on paper towels. Place 1–2 tablespoons of filling into each piece of lettuce and let the guests roll their own.
Serves 4–6

Preparing Vegetables for Stir-Frying

To prepare carrots and courgettes (zucchini, baby marrows) first cut them into thin slices.	*Stack several slices together and cut into strips the size of a match.*	*Core and cut pepper (capsicum, bell pepper) into four then slice into sticks the size of a match.*	*Slice celery diagonally.*

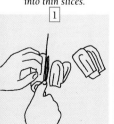
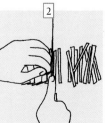
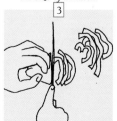
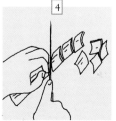

Sliced Steak with Chinese Cabbage

Cut partially frozen steak into strips 3 cm/1¼ inches wide.	*Heat the wok, then the oil and throw in garlic, ginger and spring onion (scallion).*	*Add steak and mushrooms. Stir-fry until meat changes colour. Remove from wok.*	*Stir-fry vegetables and chestnuts until cabbage softens. Add rest of ingredients. Stir until sauce is smooth.*
1	2	3	4

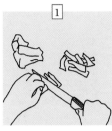 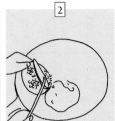 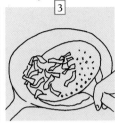 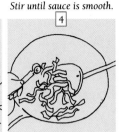

Sliced Steak with Chinese Cabbage

3 dried Chinese mushrooms
400 g/14 oz lean steak, partially frozen
3 tablespoons peanut oil
2 garlic cloves, chopped
1 piece of fresh root ginger (12 mm/½ inch), sliced
1 spring onion (scallion), chopped
¼ small Chinese cabbage, sliced
150 g/5 oz baby corn

10–15 water chestnuts, sliced
Salt
200 ml/7 fl oz/¾ cup stock
1 tablespoon oyster sauce
1 tablespoon dark soy sauce
2 teaspoons sesame oil
2 teaspoons cornflour (cornstarch)

Soak the mushrooms in cold water for 30 minutes or until soft. Drain them and remove the stalks before slicing the caps. Cut the steak across the grain into strips 3 cm/1¼ inches wide.

Heat the wok and pour in 2 tablespoons of the oil. Add the garlic, ginger and spring onion. Stir–fry these ingredients for 30 seconds before adding the steak and mushrooms. Continue to stir–fry until the meat changes colour, which should take about 3–5 minutes. Remove the steak and mushrooms from the wok.

Heat the wok again and add the remaining oil. Stir in the Chinese cabbage, baby corn and water chestnuts. Season the vegetables with salt. Continue to stir–fry for 1 minute before adding the stock. Bring the stock to the boil and cook until the cabbage starts to soften.

Return the meat and mushrooms to the wok containing the vegetables, add the oyster sauce, soy sauce and sesame oil. Dissolve the cornflour in a little water, and stir it into the meat and vegetables in the wok. Continue cooking until the liquid makes a smooth sauce. Serve with Fried Noodles (p. 35).

Serves 4–6

Sliced Steak with Chinese Cabbage has a rich flavour enhanced by the Chinese mushrooms.

The ingredients for Sliced Steak with Chinese Cabbage (p. 14) all can be prepared in advance. The dish is then quickly stir-fried in the last few minutes before serving.

Devilled Nuts

These chilli nuts are great to serve warm or cold. Once they are cooked they can be stored in an airtight container for up to a week.

6 tablespoons oil

200 g/7 oz/1¼ cups cashews

200 g/7 oz/1¼ cups pecan nuts

200 g/7 oz/1¼ cups almond kernels

1 teaspoon salt

1 teaspoon chilli powder

1 teaspoon paprika

Heat the wok and pour in half the oil. When it is really hot, add half the nuts. Stir–fry quickly for 3–4 minutes. Remove the nuts from the wok and drain well. Heat the remaining oil, add in the remaining nuts and stir–fry them for 3–4 minutes.

When all the nuts have been stir–fried and drained, combine the salt, chilli powder and paprika, and toss through the nuts; mix well to cover the nuts evenly in the chilli mixture. Serve the nuts warm, or allow them to cool and store them in an airtight container.

Chinese Cabbage Stir-Fry

Chinese cabbage has a soft, spongy texture which is ideal for absorbing the flavours of ginger and garlic.

1 tablespoon oil
1 garlic clove, chopped
1 piece of fresh root ginger (2.5 cm/1 inch), grated

½ small Chinese cabbage, finely shredded
½ teaspoon oyster sauce

Heat the wok and pour in the oil. Add the garlic and ginger, then stir–fry for 30 seconds before adding the Chinese cabbage. Now stir–fry over high heat until the cabbage starts to soften, which should take 3–4 minutes. Stir in the oyster sauce, cover and cook for a further 2–3 minutes. Serve immediately.

Serves 4

Stir-Fried Chicken and Almonds

A popular Chinese dish that is often served in restaurants. For a variation, use cashews instead of almonds, preparing them in the same way, and fold them through the cooked chicken just before serving.

MARINADE
2 teaspoons light soy sauce
1 tablespoon dry sherry
1 teaspoon cornflour (cornstarch)
1 teaspoon peanut oil

2 chicken breasts, cut into 12 mm/½ inch cubes
4 tablespoons peanut oil
60 g/2 oz/½ cup blanched almonds

125 g/4 oz/1 cup sliced French (green) beans
2 celery sticks, sliced
125 g/4 oz/¾ cup sliced bamboo shoots
200 ml/7 fl oz/¾ cup chicken stock (p. 19)
1 tablespoon oyster sauce
1 teaspoon hoisin sauce
2 teaspoons light soy sauce
2 teaspoons cornflour (cornstarch)

Combine the marinade ingredients and mix with the chicken. Cover and chill for 15 minutes.

Heat the wok and pour in half the oil. Add the almonds and stir–fry until golden brown. Remove the almonds with a slotted spoon and set aside to drain.

Add another tablespoon of oil to the wok and heat. Stir–fry the chicken pieces in the hot oil until they turn white. Remove the chicken from the wok and drain.

Pour the remaining oil into the wok and heat. Add the beans, celery and bamboo shoots, stir–fry the vegetables for a few seconds, then add the stock. Cover and cook for 3 minutes. Return the chicken to the wok and stir in the oyster, hoisin and soy sauces. Dissolve the cornflour in a little water and add it to the chicken and vegetables in the wok. Bring the liquid to the boil and cook until the liquid makes a smooth sauce.

Stir the almonds through the chicken and vegetables. Serve with steamed rice.

Serves 2–3

Stir-Fried Steak and Tomatoes

A quick, flavoursome family meal, with little preparation or cooking time. Serve with steamed rice.

400 g/14 oz lean steak, partially frozen	2 teaspoons sugar
2 tablespoons oil	2 teaspoons light soy sauce
2 garlic cloves, chopped	2 teaspoons dark soy sauce
2–3 spring onions (scallions), chopped	2 teaspoons cornflour (cornstarch)
500 g/18 oz/2½ cups chopped very ripe tomatoes	

Cut the steak across the grain into strips 3 cm/1¼ inches wide.

Heat the wok and pour in the oil. Add the garlic and spring onions and stir–fry for 30 seconds before adding the steak. Continue to stir–fry until the meat changes colour, which will take 3–5 minutes. Remove the meat from the wok and drain.

Put the tomatoes in the wok and cook them until pulpy. Add the sugar and soy sauces. Return the meat to the wok.

Dissolve the cornflour in a little water, add it to the meat and tomatoes in the wok and cook until the liquid makes a smooth sauce. Serve immediately.

Serves 4

Thai Chicken Stir-Fry

The fresh flavours of this dish will make it a favourite that you will love to present time and time again. Have everything ready; it cooks in no time.

2 tablespoons oil	2 teaspoons brown sugar
1 garlic clove, chopped	2 tablespoons chopped coriander (cilantro)
1 onion, chopped	2 tablespoons chopped mint
1 tablespoon curry powder	2 tablespoons chopped basil
4 chicken breast fillets, cut into strips	2 red chillies, chopped
2 tablespoons nam pla (fish sauce)	1 piece of fresh root ginger (2.5 cm/1 inch), grated
3 tablespoons thick coconut milk (p. 20)	1 tablespoon chopped lemon grass
1 tablespoon lemon juice	Chopped spring onions (scallions), to garnish

Heat the wok and pour in the oil. Add the garlic, onion and curry powder; stir–fry for 1 minute. Stir in the chicken and continue stir–frying until the chicken changes colour.

Add the nam pla, coconut milk, lemon juice, brown sugar, coriander, mint, basil, chilli, ginger and lemon grass to the wok. Cook for a further 2 minutes, stir–frying and moving the chicken all the time. Serve garnished with spring onions and accompanied by steamed jasmine rice and plenty of China tea.

Serves 4–6

Preparing Crabs

Hold the crab and break off the large claw. Crack it with a hammer.	*Use your thumb to prize open the shell.*	*Break the body into two. Crack it. Discard the shell and gills.*	*The crab is now broken into the claws, two halves of the body, and the roe.*

  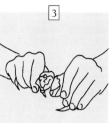 

Chilli Crab

A traditional dish from Singapore, Chilli Crab is served in a rich tomato sauce spiked with ginger, garlic and chilli. Finger bowls and plenty of napkins are a must to include on the table when serving this dish.

2 x 400 g/14 oz raw crabs
125 ml/4 fl oz/½ cup peanut oil
1 piece of fresh root ginger (2.5 cm/1 inch), grated
2 garlic cloves, chopped
3 red chillies, chopped

3 tablespoons tomato sauce
3 tablespoons chilli sauce
1 tablespoon sugar
1 tablespoon light soy sauce
Salt

Cut the crabs in half (see above), and crack the nippers with a nutcracker or mallet. Heat the wok and pour in the oil. When the oil is really hot, add the crabs. Stir–fry until the crabs change colour, then remove them and drain off any excess oil.

Put the ginger, garlic and chillies into the wok and stir–fry these for 1–2 minutes or until the garlic is lightly browned. Stir in the tomato sauce, chilli sauce, sugar, soy sauce and salt. Bring to the boil. Return the crabs to the sauce and simmer for 2–3 minutes. Serve with steamed rice.

Serves 4

Chicken Stock

A good stock is the basis of many dishes and sauces. Keep a ready supply in the freezer. To make chicken stock, put 1.25 kg/2¾ lb of chicken bones and veal bones, 1 teaspoon of peppercorns, 1 onion, 1 carrot, 2 celery sticks and a bouquet garni into a large saucepan. Pour in just enough water to cover the bones. Bring to the boil slowly and keep skimming the surface to remove all the scum and make the stock clear. Simmer gently for 3 hours. Add salt to taste. Strain the stock into a bowl and, when it is cool, put it in the refrigerator. Remove the surface fat when it sets solid. Freeze the stock if it is not required within 5 days.

Thai Beef Stir-Fry

Another quick, tasty Thai dish that can be prepared in advance—the cooking will take only a few minutes.

2 tablespoons oil

800 g/1¾ lb lean steak, cut into thin, flat strips

1 piece of fresh root ginger (2.5 cm/1 inch), sliced

2 red chillies, chopped

3 lime leaves, shredded

3 tablespoons chopped coriander (cilantro)

250 g/9 oz broccoli

200 g/7 oz mangetout (snow peas)

1 red pepper (capsicum, bell pepper), cut into cubes

10 spring onions (scallions), cut into 5 cm/2 inch lengths

2 teaspoons nam pla (fish sauce)

200 ml/7 fl oz/¾ cup thick coconut milk (p. 20)

Heat the wok and pour in the oil. Add the meat and stir–fry until the meat is well sealed, which should take 2–3 minutes. Add the ginger, chillies, lime leaves and coriander. Next add the broccoli, mangetout, red pepper and spring onions. Continue to stir–fry for a further minute. Drizzle the nam pla over the vegetables and stir in the coconut milk. Continue to stir–fry, moving all the ingredients around the wok over a high heat for 2–3 minutes. Serve immediately with plenty of steamed jasmine rice (p. 30).

Serves 6

Coconut Milk

You can make coconut milk from freshly grated coconut and freeze the leftover grated coconut or milk if the whole quantity is not required. When buying a coconut, shake it to make sure it has plenty of liquid in it and is therefore fresh. Crack it in half. (The liquid is not used except as a drink.) Prise the coconut flesh from the skin and wash it. Grate the flesh in a food processor. To make thick coconut milk, pour 300 ml/½ pint/ 1¼ cups of boiling water over 175 g/6 oz/2 cups of grated coconut and leave to stand for 5 minutes. Strain it through a sieve lined with a piece of muslin (cheesecloth). Press well to squeeze out all the liquid. Makes about 300 ml/½ pint/1¼ cups.

Slicing and Chopping

Slice ginger into thin, even pieces with a very sharp knife.

To slice a leek, slit it open with a knife, open the layers out flat and cut into thin strips.

To dice them, cut horizontally across leek and ginger strips.

When ingredient is cylindrical like a cucumber cut it into sections, then slice finely.

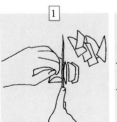

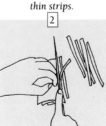

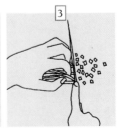

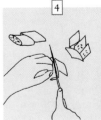

When cooking this Thai Beef Stir-Fry, the nam pla and coconut milk are added during the last few minutes.

Chicken and Mango Stir-Fry

This recipe uses the process known as 'velveting', which makes the chicken white and fluffy and helps to eliminate the problem of the chicken becoming dried out in the cooking process.

chicken breast fillets, cut into 12 mm/½ inch cubes

VELVETING
salt and pepper
teaspoon sesame oil
tablespoon oil
tablespoon dry sherry
tablespoon cornflour

2 tablespoons oil
4 spring onions (scallions), sliced
125 g/4 oz mangetout (snow peas)
2 firm mangoes, peeled and sliced
2 tablespoons chicken stock (p. 19)

To 'velvet' the chicken, place it in a bowl, stir in the velveting ingredients, mix well and allow to stand for 10 minutes.

Heat the wok and pour in the oil. When the oil is very hot, stir–fry the chicken until it changes colour. Add the spring onions, mangetout, mangoes and stock. Stir–fry for a further 2 minutes, then serve immediately.

Serves 2–3

Stir-Fried Chicken Teriyaki

Teriyaki is a Japanese dish made up of chicken, meat or seafood. The food is marinated in soy sauce and mirin and is traditionally grilled (broiled)–in Japanese 'teri' means sunshine and 'yaki' means to grill (broil). This stir-fried version is quick and equally delicious.

4 tablespoons oil

4 tablespoons light soy sauce

2 tablespoons honey

1 tablespoon mirin or dry sherry

2 garlic cloves, chopped

1 piece of fresh root ginger (2.5 cm/1 inch), grated

1 teaspoon dry mustard

4 chicken fillets, cut into 2.5 cm/1 inch strips

125 g/4 oz mangetout (snow peas)

90 g/3 oz/½ cup sliced bamboo shoots

3 spring onions (scallions), sliced

Place the oil, soy sauce, honey, mirin or sherry, garlic, ginger and dry mustard in a large bowl, mix well. Stir the chicken into this marinade and coat well. Cover and chill for 1–2 hours.

Drain the chicken from the marinade and pour half the marinade into a heated wok. Add the drained chicken and stir–fry for 3–4 minutes or until the chicken changes colour. Add the mangetout, bamboo shoots and spring onions and continue to stir–fry for a further 1–2 minutes or until the chicken is tender.

Serves 4

Stir-Fried Chicken with Lime Juice

The addition of lime juice gives this dish a fresh, clean finish.

1 tablespoon oil

3 onions, thinly sliced

1 red chilli, sliced

1 red pepper (capsicum, bell pepper), thinly sliced

1 green pepper, thinly sliced

2 chicken breast fillets, cut into 2.5 cm/1 inch strips

3 tablespoons sugar

3 tablespoons light soy sauce

3 tablespoons lime juice

Heat the wok and pour in the oil. Add the onion and chilli and cook until the onion is transparent. Add the peppers and chicken. Continue to stir-fry for 4–5 minutes. Add the sugar and stir until it has dissolved. Reduce the heat and add the soy sauce and lime juice. Simmer for 2–3 minutes over a low heat. Serve immediately.

Serves 2–3

Spiced Pork Stir-Fry

The flavour of the fresh coriander gives this spiced pork a wonderful clean, spicy flavour. Serve it either with a green salad or with steamed rice and other Thai dishes.

450 g/1 lb pork fillet, cut into 2.5 cm/1 inch cubes

2 tablespoons light soy sauce

Pepper

2 garlic cloves, chopped

2 tablespoons hot chilli sauce

3 tablespoons lemon juice

1 tablespoon peanut oil

2 tablespoons chopped coriander (cilantro)

Place the pork in a large bowl. Combine the soy sauce, pepper, garlic, chilli sauce and lemon juice, mix these well and pour the combined marinade ingredients over the pork. Cover and leave to stand for 2 hours or overnight.

Heat the wok and add the peanut oil. Drain the pork from the marinade and put it into the hot oil. Stir-fry for 3–4 minutes or until the pork is tender. Serve sprinkled with the chopped coriander.

Serves 4

Left: Stir-Fried Chicken Teriyaki cooking in the wok and about to be served.

Overleaf: Garnished with the traditional Thai coriander, this finished Thai Beef Stir-Fry (p. 20) is ready to eat.

Szechwan Chicken Stir-Fry

*The Szechwan (Sichuan) region of China is known for its use of ginger, garlic and its fiery peppercorns.
Szechwanese food blends spiciness with flavour. The seasonings are designed to make the people perspire and
stimulate the taste-buds in the hot, humid weather.*

5 tablespoons light soy sauce

2 tablespoons white wine vinegar

2 tablespoons sugar

½ teaspoon ground cayenne pepper

3 tablespoons cornflour (cornstarch)

4 chicken breast fillets, cut into 2.5 cm/1 inch cubes

2 tablespoons oil

2 garlic cloves, chopped

1 piece of fresh root ginger (12 mm/½ inch), grated

4 spring onions (scallions), sliced

Combine the soy sauce, vinegar, sugar and cayenne in a small bowl. Place the cornflour in a
paper or polythene bag, add the chicken and shake the bag to coat the chicken in flour. Heat the
wok and pour in the oil. Add the garlic and ginger stir-fry for 30 seconds before adding the coated chicken. Stir–fry until the chicken changes colour. Add the combined soy sauce mixture and
the spring onions. Stir–fry a further minute before serving.
Serves 4

Stir-Fried Beef Satay

*Satays originated in Malaysia. The spiced meat or chicken is usually threaded on to skewers and grilled, but
this stir-fried version is delicious in a hot spicy peanut sauce. Serve with plenty of steamed rice to mop up the sauce.*

1 kg/2¼ lb fillet of beef, partially frozen

2 tablespoons light soy sauce

2 garlic cloves, chopped

1 teaspoon sesame oil

5 tablespoons vegetable oil

Salt and pepper

2 onions, sliced

1 tablespoon satay sauce

1 tablespoon oyster sauce

1 teaspoon chilli sauce

3 tablespoons beef stock

2 teaspoons chopped coriander (cilantro)

Cut the beef fillet into thin slices across the grain. Combine the soy sauce, garlic, sesame oil,
3 tablespoons of the vegetable oil, salt and pepper in a large bowl. Stir the beef slices into this
marinade and leave to stand for at least 30 minutes.

Heat the wok and pour in the remaining oil. Add the drained beef and stir–fry for 2–3
minutes. Remove the beef from the wok and put in the onions. Stir–fry for 1–2 minutes or until
transparent. Add the three sauces and the stock and stir well over a medium heat until well
combined. Return the beef to the sauce and stir to coat in the sauce. Cover the wok with a lid
and cook a further 1–2 minutes over a medium heat. Sprinkle with coriander before serving.
Serves 4–6

Satay Sauce

300 ml/½ pint/1¼ cups oil
125 g/4 oz/¾ cup shelled peanuts
6 red chillies, chopped
2 garlic cloves, chopped
1 onion, chopped

Salt
Juice of 2 lemons
250 ml/8 fl oz/1 cup water
3 tablespoons brown sugar
1 teaspoon shrimp paste

Heat the oil in the wok and deep-fry the peanuts until they start to brown and take on a roasted aroma. Remove the peanuts from the oil and drain well on paper towels. Place the drained peanuts, chillies, garlic, onion, salt and lemon juice in a food processor and process until a thick paste is formed.

Remove oil and return 3 tablespoonsful to the wok. Add the peanut paste to the remaining oil and cook for about 1 minute, stirring well. Stir in the water, brown sugar and shrimp paste. Simmer the sauce gently, stirring occasionally, until the mixture thickens. Store any unused Satay Sauce, covered, in the refrigerator for later use.
Makes about 350 ml/12 fl oz/1½ cups

Chicken and Baby Corn Stir-Fry

This is a quick stir-fry using canned baby corn, which is readily available in supermarkets.

2 tablespoons oil
4 chicken breast fillets, cut into 2.5 cm/1 inch strips
2 garlic cloves, sliced
1 red pepper (capsicum, bell pepper), sliced
1 green pepper, sliced

1–2 red chillies, sliced
250 g/9 oz canned baby corn
1 tablespoon nam pla (fish sauce)
1 tablespoon light soy sauce

Heat the wok and pour in the oil. Add the chicken and stir-fry for 2–3 minutes or until the chicken changes colour. Remove the chicken from the wok;. do not put it in the refrigerator. Put the garlic, peppers and chillies into the wok and stir-fry for 30 seconds. Return the chicken to the wok along with the baby corn. Add the nam pla and soy sauce. Stir–fry the chicken, vegetables and sauces together quickly. Serve with steamed rice.
Serves 4

Dusting with Flour
The easiest and cleanest way to dust meats or poultry with flour or breadcrumbs is to put the flour or breadcrumbs into a paper bag, put the food to be coated into the bag a few pieces at a time, clutch the top of the bag closed and shake. The pieces will be evenly coated in flour or crumbs and your kitchen will be spotless.

Fried Rice

For the best result when preparing fried rice, always use long-grain rice that has been cooked and cooled. The rice should then be spread on paper towels or a cloth and allowed to dry. It is often best to cook the rice the day before and have it ready to use when you are ready to cook. Store the cooked rice in the refrigerator. This recipe is for a basic fried rice that in China would be served only in the home or to immediate family.

350 g/12 oz/2½ cups cooked long-grain rice, cooled (p. 30)
Salt and pepper

2 tablespoons peanut oil
2 eggs

Season the rice well with salt and pepper. Heat the wok and pour in the oil. When the oil is really hot, add the rice. Cook over a gentle heat, stirring continuously, for about 10 minutes or until all the oil has been absorbed.

Beat the eggs to a smooth mixture. Pour the beaten egg on to the rice in a thin stream. Continue stir–frying to mix the egg through the hot rice and allow it to set. Cook until the egg is evenly mixed and set. Serve immediately.

Serves 4–6

Fried Rice with Pork and Prawns (Shrimp)

The addition of pork and prawns make this fried rice a nutritious light meal if served on its own. It can also be served with a selection of other dishes for a more substantial meal or as part of a buffet or banquet.

2 tablespoons oil
2 spring onions (scallions), chopped
1 garlic clove, chopped
350 g/12 oz/2½ cups cooked long-grain rice, cooled (p.30)

175 g/6 oz/1½ cups chopped cooked pork
125 g/4 oz cooked prawns (shrimp)
2 tablespoons light soy sauce
2 eggs
Salt and pepper

Heat the wok and add the oil. When the oil is really hot, stir–fry the spring onions and garlic for a few seconds before adding the rice, chopped pork, prawns and soy sauce. Stir–fry until the oil is absorbed and the mixture is well mixed together.

Beat the eggs with a fork until they form a smooth mixture; season well with salt and pepper. Pour the beaten egg on to the rice and other ingredients in the wok in a thin stream. Continue to stir–fry, moving all the ingredients around the wok to mix the egg through the hot rice and allow it to set. Serve immediately.

Serves 4–6

This simple Fried Rice can be served on its own, or as part of a meal with one or two other dishes.

Deep-Frying

Food that has been properly deep-fried has a light, crisp texture.

When using a wok for deep-frying, there must be enough oil in the wok so that the food being cooked can be completely submerged and will not need to be turned during the cooking. However, the wok should not be more than one-third full in case the oil bubbles up when food is added.

Always use very clean oil, preferably peanut oil, because it does not easily burn at high temperatures.

The oil should be very hot (about 180°C/350°F) before adding the food, so that the food absorbs the minimum amount of fat and the food is sealed quickly.

There are several tests that can be used to determine the temperature of the oil. As most woks, except the electric types, do not have thermostats, these tests are useful to know. First, bubbles indicate that there is water present; these bubbles need to be driven off by further heating before the oil is ready for frying. A slight blue haze rises from the surface of the oil when it is heated, and as the temperature rises this haze becomes thicker; when the oil has overheated, the haze is produced very rapidly. The oil is ready when a small piece of bread dropped into the oil causes bubbling and becomes crisp and golden in about 1 minute. If there are no bubbles and the bread remains a poor colour, then the oil is not hot enough to fry in.

The food should be well dried before cooking or coating in batter, flour, pastry or bread-crumbs. The reason that deep-fried food is often coated before being fried is to protect the food from the intense heat of the oil and to prevent the nutrients from leaching from the food.

Only fry small amounts at a time, as adding too much food will reduce the temperature of the oil and the food being cooked will become soggy. Also, if too much food is added at one time it can cause excessive bubbling and the oil may run over the sides of the wok.

Deep-fried food should be well drained before serving. This is best done on paper towels.

Large pieces of meat or poultry should not be deep-fried, as they take a long time to cook and absorb too much oil.

Steamed Rice

Place 1½ cups of water and 1 cup of long-grain rice into a heavy-based saucepan and bring to the boil; stir well. Reduce the heat so that the rice is just simmering. Cover the saucepan with a tight-fitting lid and cook for 10 minutes. Remove the rice from the heat and allow to stand for 10 minutes, still covered. Use a fork to fluff up the rice before serving. This recipe will give 3 cups of cooked rice. To make steamed jasmine rice, use the above recipe with long-grain jasmine-flavoured Thai rice, available in Asian food stores.

Sweet and Sour Pork

The Chinese sweet and sour pickles used in this recipe are available from Chinese supermarkets or speciality stores.

SAUCE

125 ml/4 fl oz/½ cup white vinegar

90 g/3 oz/½ cup brown sugar

½ teaspoon salt

1 teaspoon light soy sauce

1 carrot, cut into julienne strips

3 slices canned pineapple, chopped

1 teaspoon cornflour (cornstarch)

BATTER

125 g/4 oz/1 cup self-raising (self-rising) flour

1 teaspoon salt

1 egg, beaten

2 teaspoons light soy sauce

250 g/9 oz shoulder pork, cut into 2.5 cm/1 inch cubes

Oil for deep-frying

3–4 tablespoons Chinese sweet and sour pickles

First make the sauce. Combine the vinegar, brown sugar, salt and soy sauce in a small saucepan. Place over a gentle heat and stir until the sugar has dissolved. Add the carrot and pineapple and allow to simmer for 1–2 minutes. Dissolve the cornflour in a little water and stir it into the sauce. Continue to stir the sauce until it thickens; allow it to boil for 1 minute.

To make the batter, sift the flour and salt into a bowl, add the beaten egg and sufficient water to achieve a thick consistency. Place the pork in the batter.

Heat sufficient oil in the wok to deep-fry the pork a few pieces at a time. To stop the pieces from sticking together during the frying, add the pork to the oil one piece at a time. Fry until the pork is golden, then remove it and drain well on paper towels.

Mix the cooked pork with the sauce and place on a heated serving dish. Garnish with sweet and sour pickles. Serve steamed rice separately.

Serves 4–6

The preparation of Mini Spring Rolls (p. 33) makes a pleasant, relaxing task.

The combination of lightly stir-fried vegetables, encased in the crisp texture of lightly fried spring roll wrappers, makes these Mini Spring Rolls (p. 33) a favourite for snacks and parties.

Omelettes

Omelettes are often used in Asian cooking to garnish dishes, especially rice. The omelette is made from beaten egg, with sometimes a little water added just before cooking to make the omelette lighter. The omelette is cooked in the wok. It is then rolled up and sliced for use.

Making Spring Rolls

Stir-fry the vegetables until they soften.

Place a tablespoon of vegetable mixture at one end of the spring roll wrapper.

Fold the sides of the wrapper in and brush the end lightly with egg white.

Roll spring rolls up firmly around the filling.

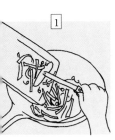
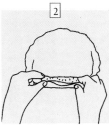
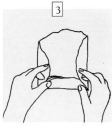
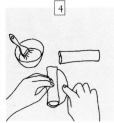

Mini Spring Rolls

These are great for parties or when serving drinks. Make up a batch and freeze them, ready to cook when unexpected guests arrive.

1 tablespoon oil
1 garlic clove, chopped
1 red chilli, chopped
200 g/7 oz can bamboo shoots, sliced into thin strips
2 carrots, sliced into thin strips
2 celery sticks, sliced into thin strips

125 g/4 oz bean sprouts
1 teaspoon chilli sauce
20 small spring roll wrappers
1 egg white, beaten
Oil for deep-frying

Heat the wok and pour in the oil. Add the garlic and chilli and stir–fry for 30 seconds, then add the bamboo shoots, carrots, celery and bean sprouts. Continue to stir–fry for 3–4 minutes or until the vegetables begin to soften. Stir in the chilli sauce and allow the mixture to cool for 30 minutes.

Place a tablespoon of the mixture on one end of a spring roll wrapper, fold the sides of the wrapper in and brush the end lightly with egg white. Roll up firmly around the filling. Continue making the spring rolls until all the filling is used.

Heat sufficient oil in the wok to deep-fry the spring rolls a few at a time. After frying, drain the spring rolls well on paper towels. Serve with chilli dipping sauce.

Chilli Dipping Sauce
125 ml/4 fl oz/½ cup light soy sauce
½ red chilli, chopped

1 tablespoon chilli sauce
Pinch of ground ginger

Combine all the ingredients for the sauce and mix well.

Tempura

Tempura is a favourite Japanese dish. The crisp, light, almost transparent batter is suitable for a variety of foods, but it needs to be served immediately it is cooked.

1 egg
1 tablespoon peanut oil
250 ml/8 fl oz/1 cup iced water
90 g/3 oz/¾ cup plain (all–purpose) flour
Pinch of bicarbonate of soda (baking soda)

Peanut oil for deep-frying
Selection of the following: button mushrooms, sliced
    courgettes (baby marrows, zucchini), asparagus,
    red and green pepper (capsicum, bell pepper),
    prawns (shrimp), fish pieces.

Place the egg, oil and water in a mixing bowl; whisk until combined. Sift together the flour and bicarbonate of soda and whisk into the egg mixture to make a smooth batter.

Heat sufficient oil in the wok to deep-fry a few pieces of tempura at a time. Dip the selected food into the batter and fry until golden brown. Drain on paper towels and serve immediately.

A Japanese soy sauce or a dipping sauce is usually served with tempura.

Serves 4

Fried Pork Balls with Courgettes (Zucchini)

The pork balls used in this recipe can also be served with Chilli Dipping Sauce (p. 33).

2 dried Chinese mushrooms
25 dried prawns (shrimp)
450 g/1 lb/4 cups minced (ground) pork
2 teaspoons light soy sauce
3 teaspoons cornflour (cornstarch)
Pinch each of salt and sugar

Plain (all–purpose) flour
Oil for deep-frying
450 g/1 lb courgettes (baby marrows, zucchini),
    cut into julienne strips
125 ml/4 fl oz/½ cup chicken stock (p. 19)
1 tablespoon dark soy sauce

Soak the mushrooms and prawns in cold water for about 30 minutes or until soft, then cut the mushrooms finely using a sharp knife. Combine the minced pork with the mushrooms, stir in the light soy sauce, 2 teaspoons of cornflour, and the salt and sugar. Moisten your hands lightly with water and, taking 1 tablespoon of pork mixture at a time, roll the mixture into small balls. Coat the balls lightly with flour. Heat sufficient oil in the wok to deep-fry a few pork balls at a time. Fry the pork balls for 3–5 minutes. Drain them well on paper towels.

Remove all but 1 tablespoon of oil from the wok and add the courgettes. Stir–fry for 1 minute before adding the chicken stock, then cook a further 2–3 minutes. Add the cooked pork balls along with the dark soy sauce. Dissolve 1 teaspoon of cornflour in a little water and stir it into the pork and courgettes. Cook until the liquid forms a smooth sauce.

Serves 4–6

Cleaned and butterflied green prawns (shrimp), ready to be fried and finished in honey to make delicious Honey Prawns (Shrimp) (p. 36).

Fried Noodles

125 g/4 oz Chinese dried noodles   125 ml/4 fl oz/½ cup peanut oil

Soak the noodles in hot water for 20 minutes, then loosen them with a fork. Drain and leave to stand for 2 hours.

Heat the wok and add the oil. When the oil is very hot, fry the noodles until both sides are slightly crisp. Drain well on paper towels before serving.

Serves 3–4

Deep-Frying Meatballs

Combine the minced pork with the mushrooms and stir in soy, flour, salt and sugar.	*Moisten hand and roll pork mixture into small balls, using a tablespoonful for each ball.*	*Heat the wok and the oil and deep-fry a few balls at a time.*	*Remove with a slotted spoon and drain on paper towels.*
1	2	3	4

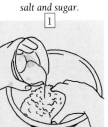
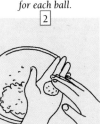
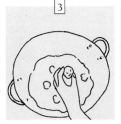
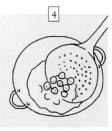

Honey Prawns (Shrimp)

These prawns are always a favourite. Try coating them with a different type of nut each time you cook the dish, to change the flavour. A handy hint to remember when measuring out honey is to heat the spoon before dipping it into the honey, so that the honey runs easily off the spoon.

450 g/1 lb green prawns (shrimp)
60 g/2 oz/½ cup cornflour (cornstarch)
90 g/3 oz/¾ cup plain (all–purpose) flour
½ teaspoon salt
2 eggs, beaten

Oil for deep-frying
3 tablespoons honey dissolved in 125 ml/4 fl oz/
   ½ cup hot water
Chopped nuts (walnuts, almonds, pecans) or
   sesame seeds

Peel the prawns and remove the intestinal vein. With a small sharp knife cut along the back of the prawns so that they open out like a butterfly when they are cooked. Sprinkle the cleaned prawns with a little of the cornflour.

Sift the plain flour and remaining cornflour and salt into a mixing bowl. Gradually add the beaten eggs and enough of the cold water to make a thin batter. Let the batter stand for 15 minutes before using.

Heat sufficient oil in the wok to deep-fry the prawns a few at a time. When the oil is hot, coat the prawns lightly with batter and deep-fry a few at a time until golden brown. Remove from the oil and drain well on paper towels.

When all the prawns have been fried and drained, remove oil. Return 2 tablespoons oil to wok, reduce the heat and quickly stir in the dissolved honey. Return the prawns to the wok and stir well to coat in the honey mixture. Lift the prawns out on to a plate that contains the chopped nuts or sesame seeds. Evenly coat the prawns with nuts or seeds.
Serves 4

Butterfly Prawns (Shrimp)

| Remove head and shell of prawn, leaving the tail intact. | Split along the back with a sharp knife. | Devein the prawn by pulling out the intestine with a toothpick or a skewer. | Wash and dry the prawns and they are ready to cook. |

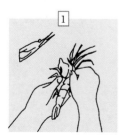
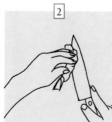
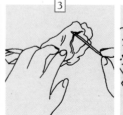
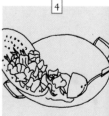

Honey Prawns (Shrimp) finish cooking in a honey syrup before being tossed in sesame seeds or chopped nuts.

Step by Step

Steaming

S teaming is cooking food in the steam of a boiling liquid. It is a slower method of cooking than boiling.

There are several ways of using a wok for steaming. You can put the food in a bamboo steamer basket, which is used in China and many Asian countries. You can use a plate placed on a rack over the boiling liquid. You can place the food in a bowl and sit the bowl in the boiling water. Whichever way you choose to steam food in your wok, you will need a fairly tight-fitting lid for the wok.

When steaming, the water must be kept boiling all the time so that the heat is at a constant temperature.

There should be no loss of steam during the cooking. The lid should fit the wok tightly.

Some foods need to be covered during the steaming to prevent the top surface of the food becoming soggy. This can be done by covering the food with a damp cloth or greaseproof (waxed) paper.

Steamed Seafood Mousse (p. 40) requires lengthy preparation, but there is nothing else to do once the ingredients are mixed and placed in the steamer.

Steamed Velvet Chicken with Lemon Sauce

This dish is of Thai origin, but it also uses the Chinese technique of 'velveting' the chicken, to keep the chicken moist and full of flavour. In this recipe the chicken is steamed instead of being stir-fried. Serve with steamed rice and stir-fry vegetables.

VELVETING

2 egg whites

2 tablespoons cornflour (cornstarch)

2 tablespoons mirin or dry sherry

½ teaspoon salt

2 tablespoons oil

900 g/2 lb chicken fillets, cut into 2.5 cm/
  1 inch cubes

4 tablespoons hoisin sauce

2–3 tablespoons black bean paste

2 tablespoons light soy sauce

2 tablespoons mirin or dry sherry

2 teaspoons sugar

Salt

2 tablespoons lemon juice

Grated rind of 1 lemon

2 tablespoons vegetable oil

Thin lemon slices

Combine all the velveting ingredients and mix well. Stir the chicken into this mixture until well coated, then cover and allow to stand for 10 minutes.

Remove the chicken pieces and spread them evenly on a heatproof plate.

Mix together the hoisin sauce, black bean paste, soy sauce, sherry or mirin, sugar, salt, lemon juice and rind and oil until smooth. Spoon this sauce over the chicken and surround with the lemon slices.

Put the plate into a bamboo steamer. Pour 5 cm/2 inches of water into the base of the wok and bring to the boil. Place the steamer in the wok and cover with a tight-fitting lid. Steam for 20–30 minutes or until the chicken is tender.

Serves 4–6

Steaming

If possible, use a bamboo steamer which will fit in a wok over boiling water.	Inside the steamer place a bowl containing the item to be cooked.	If you do not have a steamer, place a bowl in boiling water in the wok.	The wok should have a tight-fitting lid for this method.

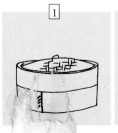

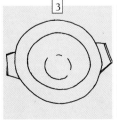

Steamed Seafood Mousse

A delicious mousse, the flavours coming from the curry paste that is added to the coconut milk. Make a double quantity of the curry paste and store it in the refrigerator. Not only can it be used for another Steamed Seafood Mousse, it is also delicious added to a stir-fry of chicken and vegetables. This recipe calls for leaves of the kaffir lime, a member of the citrus family. Ordinary lime leaves or lemon leaves can be substituted.

CURRY PASTE
3 red chillies, chopped
3 garlic cloves, chopped
4 spring onions (scallions), chopped
2 tablespoons finely sliced lemon grass
1 tablespoon chopped galangal
1 tablespoon kaffir lime leaves
1 tablespoon chopped coriander (cilantro)
Salt and pepper

MOUSSE MIXTURE
125 g/4 oz shelled green prawns (shrimp), chopped
125 g/4 oz squid (calamari), sliced

250 ml/8 fl oz/1 cup thick coconut milk (p. 20)
2 eggs
125 g/4 oz crab meat
1 teaspoon nam pla (fish sauce)
Pinch of sugar
3 cabbage leaves
4 tablespoons basil leaves

GARNISH
2 teaspoons coriander (cilantro) sprigs
Kaffir lime leaves, shredded
1 red chilli, sliced

Place all the curry paste ingredients in the bowl of a food processor and add a little water to moisten them. Process until all the ingredients are well blended. Transfer the mixture to a strainer and press out as much moisture from the curry paste as possible. (Any water left in the paste will spit when added to the hot oil.)

Combine the prawns and squid in a glass or china bowl and gradually blend in the coconut milk using a large spoon. When half the coconut milk has been added stir in the curry paste and then blend in the remainder of the coconut milk. Stir the eggs, crab, nam pla and sugar into the mousse mixture.

Use the cabbage leaves to line a heatproof bowl, then place the basil leaves inside the cabbage leaves. Spoon the fish mousse mixture into the prepared bowl, cover the mousse with silicone paper or greased greaseproof (waxed) paper. Pour 5 cm/2 inches of water into the base of the wok and place a wire rack or steamer basket over the water. Bring the water to the boil before placing the fish mousse in the wok. Cover the wok with a tight-fitting lid and steam the mousse until set, about 20 minutes.

To serve, sprinkle the top of the mousse with coriander, shredded lime leaves and sliced chilli. Serve steamed rice separately.

Serves 4–6

The combination of Thai spices and herbs gives this Steamed Seafood Mousse a rich, creamy texture.

The bright colours of the peppers ensure this Steamed Oriental Fish looks as good as it tastes.

Steamed Oriental Fish

Use your favourite white fish for this recipe. If you prefer to use fish fillets, then place the vegetables on top of each fillet before steaming and reduce the cooking time to suit the thickness of the fillets.

1 piece of fresh root ginger (12 mm/½ inch), grated
1 tablespoon peanut oil
1 garlic clove, sliced
2 small whole white fish
Salt and pepper

1 red pepper (capsicum, bell pepper), cut into
   julienne strips
1 green pepper, cut into julienne strips
2 spring onions (scallions), cut into julienne strips

Combine the ginger, garlic, oil, salt and pepper. Use this mixture to brush both the skin and the inside cavity of the fish. Put the peppers and spring onions in the fish cavity. Place the fish inside a bamboo steamer basket or on a plate.

Pour 5 cm/2 inches of water into the base of the wok and bring to the boil. Place the steamer basket in the wok, cover with a tight-fitting lid and steam until the flesh of the fish is white and flakes easily from the bone when tested with a fork.
Serves 2

Steaming Dim Sim

| Mix the ingredients together in a large bowl. | Place a teaspoonful of chicken mixture in the centre of each wrapper. | Brush edges of wrappers with egg white, close up and put into steamer. | Place steamer over boiling water and steam dim sim for 15–20 minutes. |

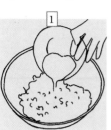 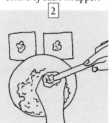 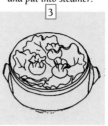 

Steamed Chicken Dim Sim

500 g/18 oz/4 ½ cups minced (ground) chicken
2 egg whites
½ teaspoon sesame oil
1 teaspoon Chinese five-spice powder
Black pepper
3 garlic cloves, chopped

1 small carrot, finely grated
125 g/4 oz/1¼ cups fresh bean sprouts
⅛ small cabbage, finely sliced
2 teaspoons light soy sauce
40 dim sim wrappers
Lettuce leaves

Combine the minced chicken, egg whites, sesame oil, spices, pepper, garlic, carrot, bean sprouts, cabbage and soy sauce in a large bowl. Mix well to blend all the ingredients together. Place a few of the dim sim wrappers on a work surface and place a teaspoonful of chicken mixture in the centre of each. Brush the edges of the wrappers with a little beaten egg white, wrap the filling in the wrappers, sealing well at the ends. Continue making dim sim in small batches until all the filling and wrappers have been used. To steam the dim sim, line a rack or a bamboo steamer with lettuce leaves and place the dim sim on the lettuce, remembering to leave some space around the dim sim to allow for swelling. Pour 5 cm/2 inches of water into the base of the wok and bring to the boil. Place the steamer on rack over the boiling water and cover the wok with a tight-fitting lid. Steam for 15—20 minutes. Serve with the Gingered Dipping Sauce.
Makes about 40

Gingered Dipping Sauce

2 teaspoons cornflour (cornstarch)
1 tablespoon brown sugar
1 piece of fresh root ginger (12 mm/½ inch), grated

1 tablespoon light soy sauce
3 tablespoons tomato sauce
3 tablespoons water

Combine the cornflour and sugar in a small saucepan. Blend together the ginger, soy sauce, tomato sauce and water; gradually stir this into the cornflour to make a smooth liquid. Stir over a gentle heat until the sauce thickens and boils. Serve warm or cold.

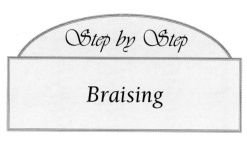

Step by Step

Braising

Braising is cooking slowly by moist heat. Meat, poultry, seafood and vegetables can all be braised in the wok.

The food is often browned in a small amount of fat and then cooked in a small amount of liquid. The wok is then covered with a tight-fitting lid and the cooking continues over a gentle heat.

Braising is often used for cheaper cuts of meat which require long, slow cooking to make them tender.

Traditionally braising was done over a bed of diced vegetables.

Braised Chicken Wings (p. 47) are served on a bed of steamed rice and garnished with lemon peel and spring onions (scallions).

Braised Seafood in Tomato Sauce

Fresh seafood cooked in a rich tomato sauce. It is simply served with crusty bread and a green salad.

1 tablespoon oil	1 tablespoon tomato paste
1 garlic clove, chopped	1 tablespoon red wine vinegar
2 white onions, chopped	2 teaspoons brown sugar
2 red chillies, chopped	500 g/18 oz green prawns (shrimp)
½ teaspoon ground cumin seed	250 g/9 oz scallops
425 g/15 oz can tomatoes	250 g/9 oz mussels

Heat the wok and pour in the oil. When the oil is hot add the garlic, onions and chillies. Stir–fry for 30 seconds, then add the cumin and tomatoes with the juice from the can. Cook until the tomatoes are pulpy. Stir in the tomato paste, vinegar and sugar. Cover the wok and simmer for 10 minutes. Add the prepared seafood and cook a further 5 minutes or until the mussels have opened, which indicates that they are cooked. Do not overcook the mussels, as they toughen easily. Discard any mussels that do not open.

Serve the seafood in large bowls with the mussels to the top.

Braised Beef and Vegetables

2 tablespoons oil	125 ml/4 fl oz/½ cup chicken stock (p. 19)
500 g/18 oz lean steak, thinly sliced	1 teaspoon oyster sauce
250 g/9 oz/2 cups sliced bamboo shoots	Salt and pepper
250 g/9 oz chopped broccoli	Pinch of sugar
425 g/15 oz can straw mushrooms, drained	1 piece of fresh root ginger (12 mm/½ inch), grated
1 teaspoon cornflour (cornstarch)	

Heat half the oil in the wok until hot. Add the beef strips and stir–fry until they are well sealed and browned; this should take 2–3 minutes. Remove the meat from the wok with a slotted spoon. Do not chill the meat.

Add the remaining oil to the wok and heat. When the oil is hot, add the bamboo shoots, broccoli and mushrooms. Stir–fry for 2 minutes.

Mix the cornflour with the stock, oyster sauce, salt and pepper, sugar and ginger. Add the cooked meat to the vegetables in the wok and add the combined cornflour mixture. Stir until the mixture boils and a smooth sauce is formed. Cover and cook for 2 minutes before serving with steamed rice.

Serves 4

Braised Chicken Wings

The lemon and ginger used in this recipe give a lovely flavour. These wings are equally good served warm or cold. When you have removed the wing tips, don't waste them, use them to make a chicken stock (p 19).

1 kg/2¼ lb chicken wings
2 tablespoons peanut oil
4 tablespoons soy sauce
2 tablespoons honey

Grated peel of 1 lemon
2 tablespoons dry sherry
1 garlic clove, chopped
1 piece of fresh root ginger (2.5 cm/1 inch), grated

Using a sharp knife, remove the wing tips from the chicken wings and cut each wing in half at the joint.

Heat the wok and pour in the oil. When the oil is very hot, add the chicken wings and stir–fry for 3–4 minutes. Stir in the soy sauce, honey, lemon peel, sherry and garlic. Keep stirring until the liquid comes to the boil. Cover the wok with a tight-fitting lid and reduce the heat. Simmer the chicken wings over a gentle heat for 30 minutes or until tender. Stir occasionally to stop the sauce from sticking, especially towards the end of the cooking time.
Serves 3–4

After the chicken wings have been stir-fried, the addition of soy, honey, lemon and sherry for the slower braising gives these Braised Chicken Wings a delicious flavour that is good both hot and cold.

Step by Step

Glossary

Bamboo shoots The young tender shoots of the bamboo plant. They are mainly used to add texture to stir–fries. They are readily available in cans.

Galangal Also known as Siamese ginger. It has a flavour between ginger and cardamom and is obtainable fresh, dried or in powdered form.

Hoisin sauce A sweet, spicy sauce made from salted soy beans, garlic, onions and spices.

Julienne vegetables Vegetables cut into thin strips (p. 13).

Kaffir lime A member of the citrus family. The leaves can also be found dried in Asian food stores.

Lemon grass An aromatic Asian plant, readily available from Asian food stores. The bulbous base is used to give a lemony flavour to Asian cooking or curries. Dried lemon grass is also available and should be soaked in hot water before use.

Marinate Soak raw ingredients in a liquid—wine, oil, vinegar, lemon juice with herbs and spices—to preserve them and to make them more tender and flavoursome.

Mirin A Japanese sweet rice wine which is low in alcohol. Dry sherry is often substituted for mirin.

Nam pla Thai fish sauce, thin and translucent, made from fish, shrimps and crabs. It is an essential ingredient in Thai cooking.

Sesame oil Oil extracted from toasted sesame seeds. It is used generally in small quantities and is usually added towards the end of the cooking. It is best to buy the Chinese sesame oil from supermarkets or Asian food stores and not the lighter coloured sesame oil sold in health food stores.

Soy sauce Made from fermented soy beans. The light sauce is usually added for flavour and is often used with white meat dishes. The dark sauce is usually added for colour and is often used with red meat dishes.

Spring roll wrappers Thin white sheets of pastry, sold frozen. Thaw and peel off the sheets one at a time before using. Refreeze any unused wrappers.

Stock Liquid made from simmering meat and vegetables in water for over three hours to extract the flavour (p. 19). Used to enhance the flavour of sauces and soups.

Water chestnuts Small, white, crisp bulbs that have a refreshing, crunchy texture for which there is no substitute. They are readily available in cans.

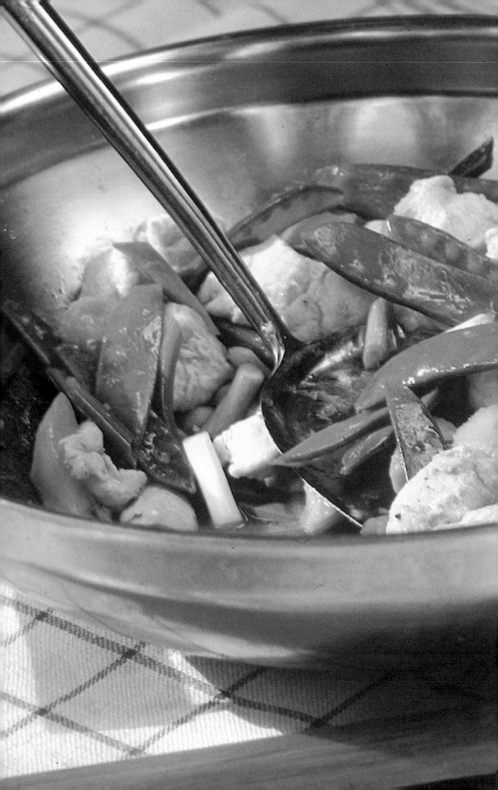